Original title:
Under the Sea's Embrace

Copyright © 2025 Creative Arts Management OÜ
All rights reserved.

Author: Penelope Hawthorne
ISBN HARDBACK: 978-1-80587-250-4
ISBN PAPERBACK: 978-1-80587-720-2

Tales from the Ocean's Whisper

In the depths a crab did dance,
Wearing shoes? Oh what a chance!
Fishy giggles all around,
Tickled scales on sandy ground.

A starfish found a cloak of shells,
Pretended to be someone else.
Seaweed swayed, I swear it smiled,
Making waves, acting wild.

A jellyfish with floppy tentacles,
Tried to juggle fishy spectacles.
Oh what a sight, a splishy splash,
Laughter bubbled in a flash.

But wait, what's that? A whale on a spree,
Trying to catch a tune from a tree!
Blowing bubbles, oh how they flew,
Making tunes like a far-off zoo.

Serenities of the Open Waters

A dolphin wore a party hat,
Inviting fishes, 'Come join my chat!'
With flips and flops, they had a ball,
Splashing joy that could enthrall.

An octopus played peek-a-boo,
With eight arms swaying to the blue.
A shy shrimp joined the funny game,
Too nervous though to ever claim fame.

A seahorse missed the morning train,
Wobbled on tracks, oh what a pain!
He sighed and said, 'I think I'll float,'
While dreaming of a captain's coat.

In finned attire, a grouper sang,
With a voice that made the water clang.
The fish gathered round, they loved his tune,
And danced beneath the cactus moon.

Deep Blue Reveries

Fins and tails in a silly chase,
Fish with hats and a smiley face.
Crabs in tuxedos, they dance quite bold,
While the goldfish gossip, their tales retold.

Mermaids giggle, flip-flop in glee,
Seaweed wigs wave like a wild spree.
Octopus juggling, what a grand sight,
As jellyfish glow in the shimmering light.

The Dance of Seafoam and Time

Sea turtles tap dance on coral reefs,
While starfish spin in their tiny briefs.
A lobster's clapping with a great big grin,
As sea slugs stomp, the party begins.

Crabby conga lines form with glee,
A dolphin pops in with a playful spree.
Seahorses twirl like they own the floor,
In this ocean ball, who could ask for more?

Beneath the Waves' Whisper

Anemones wiggle, a ticklish tease,
While clownfish laugh in the gentle breeze.
A whale sings jokes, deep in the blue,
Echoes of laughter ripple right through.

Parrots and pelicans join the fun,
In a bubble party, laughter's begun.
With sea cucumbers swaying in tune,
They're dancing away to a sunken tune.

Echoes of the Deep

Pufferfish puff at the jokes they tell,
Shrimps in bow ties rise up from their shell.
Turtles in shades wear a cool, calm smile,
While clownfish prance down the neon aisle.

Dances of angelfish, twist and loop,
A conch shell plays in the underwater troop.
With coral confetti and bubbles aglow,
The ocean's a stage for a delightful show.

The Starfish's Silent Vigil

A starfish sat on the floor,
Counting grains, it wanted more.
It wiggled arms in silent plea,
'Why can't I dance like jellyfish bee?'

Around it swirled a crab with flair,
Clipping claws, it packed a chair.
'Oh, star, just flip and take a chance,
Join us in this quirky dance!'

Echoes of the Deep Tide

In the ocean's muffled sound,
A whale sings jokes that astound.
His belly shakes with laughter bright,
As fish roll by, they take flight.

A octopus playing peek-a-boo,
Hiding in a coral brew.
With arms flailing in pure delight,
He tickles the fish, what a sight!

Anemones in Twilight's Glow

Anemones wave with graceful cheer,
Tickling fish that venture near.
'Come dance, you silly little clown!'
'Life's too fun to wear a frown!'

Surfers of bubbles, the fish parade,
Doing flips, not one afraid.
Anemones chuckle, swaying low,
Ai-ai, where'd the clownfish go?

Rippled Secrets of the Waves

Ripples giggled upon the sand,
Secrets shared from fin to hand.
'Why did the shrimp cross the tide?
To find a lobster's flip-flop slide!'

A dolphin snorted, leapt for fun,
'Come join me, everyone, everyone!'
With splashes loud, they formed a train,
'Makin' waves and jokin' again!'

The Call of the Horizon

A fish in a bowler hat, what a sight,
He dances with seaweed, it's pure delight.
A crab with sunglasses struts on the sand,
He says, 'Join my conga line, isn't it grand?'

A dolphin wearing shoes tries to sing,
But giggles and bubbles are the real thing.
A turtle in a tie flips pancakes with flair,
The ocean's a party, if you dare to share!

Shadows of the Deep Blue

In the depths, a squid plays charades with the light,
While starfish debate if it's day or night.
An octopus juggles shells, can't drop a thing,
The seaweed's in stitches—it's starting to swing.

A blowfish tries tango, puffing with pride,
But his dance moves send fishies all off to hide.
The sea-floor's a stage, every creature a star,
In this wacky wonderland, laughter travels far.

Surreal Selkie Serenade

A selkie sings loudly, but can't hit the notes,
Her sea pals all chuckle, 'Oh, dear, oh, floats!'
An otter rides waves, wearing floaties just right,
He calls out, 'Help me, I'm way too polite!'

A narwhal shows off his sparkly horn,
Claims it's an ice cream cone, a tale newly born.
With each silly giggle, they all join the spree,
In this world of wonder, everyone's free!

Murmurs of the Ocean Floor

The lobsters are gossiping, claws all aflail,
'Did you hear about the clam? He's told quite a tale!'
A seahorse in pajamas is snoozing away,
Dreaming of treasure maps and bright, jazzy days.

The jellyfish jive, with their glowing parade,
While frisky young shrimp dance a crabby charade.
The ocean hums softly, all creatures unite,
In this whimsical realm, everything feels right.

Seafoam Chronicles

A crab in a tux, what a sight!
He twirls and he shimmies, oh what a delight!
With shells as his dance floor, he glides with glee,
While fish shake their fins, saying, 'Look at me!'

The sea urchins giggle, they poke and they prod,
While dolphins in sunglasses give nods full of laud.
Octopus juggles with pearls, oh what a show!
Even the clams join in, don't you know?

A Dance with the Tides

The waves do the cha-cha, splashing around,
As starfish do the worm on the sandy ground.
Sea turtles slide by with their laid-back groove,
Making all the sea critters find their own move.

A jellyfish waltz, floating with grace,
While a seahorse prances—oh what a face!
They giggle and gurgle, the party's alive,
In this salty soiree, the fish come to thrive!

Mysteries of the Marine World

Though deep in the blue, secrets are kept,
A fish in a hat claims he's never wept.
With a wink and a splash, he tells silly tales,
Of mermaids with lasers and talking snails.

The clinking of shells tells a joke to behold,
Of a whale that wore spectacles, quite bold!
A crab with a mustache shares wisdom, you see,
'Don't take life too seriously; just let it be!'

Beneath a Blanket of Seaweed

Beneath fronds of green, where the giggles resound,
Lies a party of fish, all dancing around.
Sea cucumbers groove with a slinky-like sway,
While anemones laugh, joining in on the play.

A lobster in shades claims he's king of the reef,
With a crown made of shells, it's beyond belief!
Sand dollars cheer as they shimmy on by,
What a ridiculous scene beneath the blue sky!

The Siren's Lullaby

When fish begin to dance and twirl,
A clam began to sing a whirl.
The octopus lost its shoes,
While a crab read funny news.

Turtles try to flip and flop,
Making jokes that never stop.
A dolphin laughs, a whale's in shock,
As seahorses rock 'round the clock.

Mysteries of the Deep Blue

In the depths where strange things glow,
A fish wears glasses, don't you know?
A jellyfish with a smart phone,
Taking selfies all alone.

Pirates searching for their socks,
Finding treasure, but just rocks!
A lobster's telling knock-knock jokes,
As bubbles rise from laughing folks.

Beneath the Cascading Aquamarine

Octopus with a ukulele,
Sings of snacks—like fruit and jelly.
A school of fish throws a bash,
While sea cucumbers just smash.

Clownfish painting polka dots,
While starfish search for tiny pots.
The seaweed sways to the beat,
As crabs rock out on tiny feet.

Enchanted by the Ocean's Breath

Anemones dance in funny hats,
Tangled up with friendly spats.
A seagull tries to tell a tale,
But splashes down; it gets impaled!

Mermaids trading glossy shells,
With jokes that ring like rusty bells.
A whale flips high, the crowd goes wild,
While a fish pouts, feeling mild.

Shadows of the Ocean Depths

A crab wore a hat, oh so grand,
With sunglasses perched, looking quite planned.
He danced to the beat of a jellyfish tune,
While seahorses giggled, under the moon.

A starfish was lost, without a GPS,
Pointed three ways, caused quite the mess.
The fish rolled their eyes, what a sight to see,
As he just kept flipping, like he was on spree.

Serenade of the Underbelly

An octopus juggled, with eight flailing arms,
While a clam clapped to show its charms.
A whale low-key rapped, with beats from the swell,
And all of the fish went under his spell.

A shrimp wore a bow tie, so classy you'd think,
While seagulls plotted how to steal a drink.
The crabs put on shows, such comedic relief,
In this watery world, all shared in belief.

Still Waters, Deep Stories

A fish told a tale, of the one that got away,
Which only grew bigger with each passing day.
A goby winked slyly, with a toothy grin,
Said, "That's not the story; it's time to begin!"

A turtle was knitting, a scarf in the breeze,
With colors of kelp and a few extra leaves.
The fish gathered round, for stories and laughs,
In bright bubbles of joy, they forgot their gaffs.

Whispers in the Dolphin's Wake

Dolphins played tag, with giggles and flips,
While fishes just watched, shaking their lips.
A sea turtle sighed, 'What a ruckus today!'
As the dolphins dashed off, all ready to play.

A mermaid hiccupped, from laughter not drink,
She swam in circles, oh what a pink stink!
The sea was a circus, full of wacky grace,
With laughter and bubbles, it's the best kind of space.

Deep Stories

A grouper tried cooking, with a pinch and a dash,
He made quite the mess, in a colorful splash.
A tuna swam by, quite the gourmet,
Said, 'Let's not eat fish; let's order some hay!'

A flounder who flipped, was quite on the fence,
Whether to join in or just take offense.
But laughs filled the foam, as they dined on the hype,
In the depths of the ocean, where all are the type.

Dreams in Aquamarine

Bubbles rise with giggling fish,
A crab attempts to make a wish.
Stars are bright in waters deep,
As oysters play tag and dolphins leap.

Snails wear hats, quite the display,
Seahorses dance in a quirky way.
A clam sings loud, but flat and free,
While jellyfish waltz with glee.

Mermaids joke, their laughter loud,
As squids perform for a cheering crowd.
The ocean's laughter, a joyful sound,
In this sea of dreams, fun's found all around.

The Voyage of Lost Souls

A ghostly ship with a silly crew,
Whales play cards, oh what a view!
The captain's hat is on a fish,
As they navigate in a jelly-filled dish.

The anchor's tied to a dancing stone,
While octopuses give it moans and groans.
A parrot lost, with no sense of time,
Sings sea shanties — but can't find the rhyme.

They toast with kelp in cups of sand,
With a a pirate's laugh, so unplanned.
Ghosts do the cha-cha, just for kicks,
In waters where humor's the magic mix.

Starlit Pathways Underwater

Starfish twirl, so light and bright,
As they boogie through the moonlit night.
Anemones tickle, making fish giggle,
With every swish, they dance and wiggle.

Sardines form lines, oh what a sight!
Disco balls made of corals ignite.
A hermit crab juggling shells just for fun,
While dance-offs happen 'til the rising sun.

The mermen laugh as they trip on algae,
Chasing each other through paths so snazzy.
With every splash, the sea turns bright,
A satire of joy in the deep ocean light.

Currents of Enchantment

In a swirl of colors, fish take flight,
A turtle forgets where he left his light.
The jokes of eels, so shockingly punny,
Tickling the octopus, oh so funny!

A pufferfish poofs, just for flair,
As clowns in bubbles float in the air.
Barrels of laughs from barnacles bound,
As laughter echoes all around.

Starfish are comedians, so absurd,
With tales of crabs that are quite unheard.
In this ocean of giggles, so grand and bright,
Where the currents of joy swirl day and night.

Beneath Waves of Gold and Silver

Dancing fish in a swirling waltz,
Wearing seaweed hats, they never halt.
A crab with a cane struts with flair,
As jellyfish giggle without a care.

Starfish blush in the sandy glow,
While octopuses juggle their show.
A clam sings loudly, though tone is wrong,
As bubbles burst, they all join along.

Anemones sway like they're in a club,
While snails slide in, a very slow hub.
With laughter echoing off every shell,
The ocean's a circus - oh what a swell!

So come take a dip where the laughter swells,
Among quirky fish with their funny tales.
In this watery world, you'll not want to leave,
With creatures so silly, it's hard to believe!

Echoing Heartbeats of the Deep

A whale's voice booms like a loud old clock,
While dolphins giggle and tease with a shock.
Sea turtles nod at the crabs so spry,
"What's the rush?" they say, "Just let time fly!"

The sea cucumbers play hidden and seek,
Camouflaged pals lie still, not a squeak.
The pufferfish puffs up, all grand and proud,
Yet looks quite foolish beneath the crowd.

Grouper's got jokes that are oh-so fishy,
His punchlines are slightly too squishy.
With every guffaw, the waters swirl,
In laughter and joy, watch the bubbles twirl!

Echoing giggles fill every space,
The deep is a stage for an artful embrace.
Join in the fun, let worries be swept,
For in this grand dance, all secrets are kept.

The Magic of Forgotten Reefs

Coral castles shrug off the dust,
Where fish throw parties, oh what a must!
A lionfish struts with its colorful flair,
While clownfish giggle without a care.

The sea snails ride bubbles on their way,
While seahorses tango, come join the ballet!
Barnacles chatter in their old, wise way,
"Who needs land? Let's keep the blues at bay!"

Now shrimp in tuxedos serve tiny snacks,
As sea urchins laugh and lighten the cracks.
With laughter and cheer beneath coral spar,
Who knew being forgotten could be so bizarre?

So peek at the magic, let laughter unwind,
In reefs full of chuckles, joy you will find.
For every quick glance at these treasures bright,
Will fill your heart with pure delight!

The Gathering of Ocean Spirits

On a moonlit night, the sea sprites convene,
With shimmering tails and a glimmering sheen.
They dance in the currents, all merry and bright,
Spinning round moonbeams, what a groovy sight!

With a splash and a wink, the mermen arrive,
Cracking jokes as they jive, so lively, so alive!
A fish with a mustache claims the best mane,
As seagulls roll by, calling out is their game.

A clam plays a tune with an oyster's help,
While creatures of color elicit a yelp.
Each wave carries laughter, no worries in tow,
As spirits of ocean put on their grand show!

So come join the gathering, don't be shy,
Underneath the stars, let your spirit fly.
For in this ocean, with foolish delight,
You'll find endless giggles, we're up all night!

Whispers of the Tidal Deep

Fish in tuxedos dance with glee,
A crab in a top hat sips sweet tea.
They joke about the tangled weeds,
While a starfish writes its memoirs of deeds.

A dolphin juggles shells with flair,
An octopus draws a mustache in air.
The sea turtle plays the flowery flute,
As bubbles rise and giggles commute.

Seahorses laugh, they tell tall tales,
Of treasures found in pirate gales.
With mermaids singing songs of cheer,
It's a party underwater, bring the beer!

A whale joins in with booming laughs,
As jellyfish perform their graceful halves.
In this watery realm of silly sights,
Funny shenanigans fill the nights.

A Symphony of Coral Dreams

Clownfish crack jokes with each little pop,
While sea cucumbers just can't stop.
Anemones dance to the watery beat,
With rhythms that sway and jump on their feet.

A narwhal gets tangled in his own horn,
A seagull laughs until he's forlorn.
Shrimp in sunglasses chill by the reef,
As clams tell tales of a pirate's grief.

Starfish play games, they call it 'Hide!'
Where eels sneak peek, but don't want to glide.
This orchestra of quirks plays on,
Making the mundane feel like a con.

The coral croons sweet melodies,
While sand dollars giggle in gentle breeze.
With laughter echoing through the blue,
A symphony of giggles plays just for you.

The Moon's Reflection in the Abyss

A lobster moonwalks on the floor,
While fish wear wigs that they adore.
The reflection sparkles with whimsy and glee,
As laughter bubbles up from the sea.

A pufferfish tries to take a bow,
But gets stuck—oh, what a how!
Octopuses chuckle at the sight,
As sea stars cheer in pure delight.

The clowns of the ocean twirl around,
With jellyfish lanterns glowing profound.
A conch shell air horn blares its sound,
Celebrating silliness all around.

As the moon glows bright, the fun expands,
Even the seaweed joins in the bands.
Under the lights, all creatures play,
In this crazy ocean, where smiles stay.

Beneath Waves of Azure Calm

Parrots fish debate what's a meal,
While anemones giggle, revealing their feel.
Bubbles carry secrets from fishes so shy,
Impromptu concerts with each joyous sigh.

A walrus wearing socks from a store,
Tries to juggle while dodging a floor.
Crabs on skates slide in a parade,
With laughter ringing, they're not afraid.

A dolphin's joke hits everyone right,
Making waves with giggles, pure delight.
As seahorses swing, they twirl and they prance,
Drawing cheer from all in the underwater dance.

In the gentle embrace of waters so vast,
Time flies on by, each moment a blast.
With laughter swimming through coral caves,
The joy of this world is what everyone saves.

Celestial Waves and Soft Currents

In tides that twist like silly strings,
The fish wear hats and dance with flings.
Crabs play cards on sandy floors,
While turtles tell the best of tales and roars.

The jellyfish float, quite out of sync,
Bobbing to songs that make you think.
Starfish laugh, their jokes so bright,
Turn snails into stars on a moonlit night.

Seahorses prance in a wobbly dance,
With bubbles popping, they take a chance.
Octopuses juggle, with style so grand,
As seaweed sways with a wave of a hand.

In this realm of giggles and cheer,
Even the rocks wear a smile, I hear.
Life's a splash, with laughter, we see,
A bubbling underwater comedy spree.

Beneath Canopies of Sea Grass

Seaweed sways like a hip disco ball,
Fish wear sunglasses, feeling quite tall.
Crabs shuffle sideways, doing the twist,
While dolphins leap, oh, don't get them missed.

The coral wears polka dots with pride,
As sea cucumbers giggle, with nowhere to hide.
Clams snap shut, acting all shy,
But oysters' pearls are the ultimate sly.

Anemones tickle the curious fish,
With each gentle touch, they grant a wish.
Starfish play hide and seek quite well,
With whispers of laughter in the ocean swell.

Beneath this green, a party does bloom,
With clowns of the ocean sweeping the gloom.
Laughter echoes through murky lanes,
In the grass where silliness reigns.

Harmonies of the Deep Blue

Fish compose symphonies, oh what a sight,
With shrimps on violins, playing all night.
The sea turtles tap dance, oh-so-sly,
While groupers hum the tunes of the sky.

Bubble-blowers bubble, a soft serenade,
A tune sung by eels in a shimmering shade.
As the lobsters boogie, clad in fine shells,
Even the seagulls can't keep from yells.

The rhythm pulses, a current of cheer,
As whales belt out songs we hold dear.
In this watery concert, we can't help but grin,
For in the deep blue, the fun's just begun.

Every wave plays a note in this song,
Where everyone's welcome, you can't go wrong.
In the depths of the ocean, with spirits so free,
We celebrate life in playful harmony.

The Secrets of the Submerged

Octopus spies in every nook,
Taking notes like a sneaky crook.
With ink pen ready, he scribbles away,
Dishing secrets of fishy gourmet.

Anglerfish grin, with lights that provoke,
As browsing shrimp become the butt of a joke.
The parrotfish chatter in colors so bright,
Mimicking squawks in the pale moonlight.

Buried treasures, but not just gold,
Shells with stories have to be told.
With mermaids giggling, and pirates in tow,
The underworld humor continues to flow.

In this realm where laughter spills free,
A world of wonders, a sight to see.
Beneath the waves, the fun never ends,
Just oddball friendships that nature lends.

Waves of Forgotten Memories

I once lost my flip-flops, oh what a sight,
They danced with the crabs, in the moonlight.
Caught in a wave, they swam with a grin,
Now they tell tales of where they've been.

A starfish took selfies, quite the charmer,
Said, "I'm fabulous, no need for armor!"
While shells had a party and sang all night,
Echoing laughter in the pale starlight.

The jellyfish giggled, floated with glee,
"We're the disco balls, come dance with me!"
With piña coladas, the shrimp clinked their claws,
In the realm of the ocean, with no time for flaws.

As I wave goodbye to my pals in the tide,
I'll cherish this madness, with glee and with pride.
For memories shimmer like fish in a stream,
In the ridiculous dance of an oceanic dream.

The Language of Fishes

The fish have a gossip that bubbles so loud,
In colorful schools, they're quite the crowd.
With glimmering tails, they flap and they chat,
"Did you hear 'bout the turtle? She's lost her hat!"

A clownfish gave lessons on how to clown,
While a pufferfish puffed, wearing a frown.
"I just bloated again, it's happened before!"
They all broke in laughter, then danced on the floor.

Would you believe in a fishy debate?
The trout and the bass just couldn't relate,
"Who swims faster?" they argued with glee,
While the octopus shrugged, "Just let me be!"

With bubbles as jokes, and currents as fun,
The ocean's a place where no one can shun.
So toss in your worries and paddle along,
For the fish have a language that's never wrong!

In the Heart of a Conch Shell

Within a conch shell, I found a dear friend,
He recounted tales that would never end.
"Did you know about mermaids, they sing quite a tune?
One even swam with a raccoon under the moon!"

The crab chimed in, with pincers a-clack,
"A seagull once borrowed my favorite snack!
But to be honest, I don't mind the strife,
For who knew that seagulls could have such a life?"

The seaweed shared secrets, all tangled in green,
"Listen closely, my tales are fit for a queen!
Of treasure and trouble, of love in a net,
You'll swim with legends, don't place any bet!"

In a shell full of laughter, my heart felt so light,
Like bubbles in water that twinkle at night.
So if you find a conch, stop and give it a spin,
For a journey awaits, let the stories begin!

Beneath Stardust and Salt

Beneath stardust skies and saltwater scents,
Lived a dolphin who thought he could pay the rents.
He started a business, selling seaweed snacks,
To gulls and to turtles — he even got flacks!

An octopus joined with tentacles strong,
"I can help you out, let's make this a song!"
Together they'd pitch, to fishes in line,
"Buy two get one free, it's a deal so fine!"

But who could have guessed, that a seal would arrive,
With beach ball in flippers, so eager to dive?
He bought all the snacks, then ran in a flash,
Leaving the duo with only a splash.

Their venture was funny, but friendship was gold,
In the depths of the ocean, where stories unfold.
So if you swim by, take a chance and explore,
For beneath stardust and salt, there's always much more!

Currents of Forgotten Stories

Bubbles rise with tales untold,
A fish in a hat, quite bold.
He tells of a ship that sailed away,
Only to find seaweed had its say.

Crabs dance in a ragged line,
Wearing socks, oh what a sign!
The octopus plays the ukelele,
While sardines cheer and yell, "Hooray!"

Seahorses giggle, sharing jokes,
As clams crack up with silly pokes.
Turtles race in lazy glee,
To win a crown from a laughing sea.

So if you dive into the blue,
Listen close, there's fun for you.
With currents swirling to and fro,
The ocean's humor steals the show.

The Hidden Kingdom of the Kraken

In shadows lurks a playful beast,
Flinging ink like a wild feast.
He tickles sailors with his tentacle,
Making every battle just a spectacle.

With a wink, he makes ships swirl,
While mermaids giggle and twirl.
'Come play a game of catch,' he says,
As fish jump about in a joyous haze.

His kingdom's full of leafy greens,
Where lobsters wear the fanciest jeans.
The jellyfish sport silly hats,
And gossip about the latest chats.

So if you ever spot a splash,
Know it's just a kraken's bash.
Join the fun, don't be shy,
In the depths where laughter flies.

Lanterns of the Jellyfish Night

Glow, glow, in the deep blue light,
Jellyfish dancing, quite a sight.
Tickling currents in the dark,
They play and jest, oh what a lark!

With a giggle, they float by,
Tentacles waving, oh so sly.
Anemones roll their eyes,
At the jellyfish joking 'til sunrise.

Starfish laugh on a sandy seat,
Telling tales of slippery treats.
While anglerfish shine their bright glow,
Giggling softly, 'Come join the show!'

As bubbles pop in playful cheers,
The night dissolves all worries and fears.
In this lantern-lit, oceanic spree,
Laughter echoes, wild and free.

A Tapestry of Barnacles and Dreams

On rocks, where barnacles complain,
They dream of adventures, not so plain.
With barnacle hats and wishes galore,
They plot a journey to the ocean floor.

'Dive in!' cries one, covered in muck,
'Let's find treasures, or perhaps some luck!'
Sea turtles smirk, with a knowing glance,
As they prepare for an underwater dance.

Octopuses giggle, sharing dreams,
Of ice cream sundaes and chocolate streams.
They twist and turn, making a show,
While clowns of the reef join in the flow.

So here's to the dreams we weave,
In barnacle whispers, we believe.
In the depths where silly reigns,
Every joke is a pearl, unchained.

A World of Blue Shadows

The fish wear glasses, what a sight,
They read the paper, oh so bright!
Crab in a tux, feels quite refined,
Dancing with turtles, their shells aligned.

Octopus juggles pearls with glee,
While dolphins giggle at a seaweed spree.
A starfish sings off-key in a show,
And the sea gulls cheer from below!

Bubbles form jokes, they pop with a laugh,
The sea cucumbers plot their next gaffe.
Sharks play tag, a game of surprise,
While the hermit crabs wear funny ties!

In this world where joy never wanes,
Even the sea urchins dance on the lanes.
A lot of fish with not a single care,
In a blue bubble of laughter, they share.

The Depths of Solitude

In dark waters where the seaweed sways,
Lived a lonely clam, counting his days.
He tried disco moves, but slipped on his shell,
Now he dreams of his friends, whose stories he tells.

An old fish swims by, with quite the clout,
Says, 'You're not alone, come dance about!'
The clam, feeling brave, listened to the beat,
He flopped and he flipped with his giant seat.

Underneath the waves, they pitched a spree,
Crustacean conga, oh so free!
The lonely clam laughed until he turned red,
Maybe solitude's fun, with some friends led!

Soon the deep was a vibrant affair,
With laughs and cheers filling the water's air.
One silly clownfish swam 'round in delight,
Saying, 'Join the party, it's quite a sight!'

Treasures in the Midnight Tide

At midnight, the ocean holds a grand show,
With treasure chests open for all to know.
Pearls giggle while hiding beneath a rock,
And the sea urchins tickle the dock.

A mermaid with glitter is throwing a ball,
Fish in bow ties are having a ball.
Clams offer cupcakes made of fine sand,
While turtles play music from a seashell band.

The lighthouse beams on, a disco light,
Inviting all creatures to dance through the night.
Jellyfish twirl and lanterns they wear,
Floating with flair, all swirling in air!

Even a whale brings the softest tunes,
While starfish are dividing the silver spoons.
Under moonbeams, the magic does glide,
As laughter and treasures rise with the tide!

Beneath the Celestial Waters

Where lights sparkle bright in the ocean's deep,
A goldfish dreams, and the sea turtles leap.
They throw a party, with bubbles galore,
As anemones dance, who could ask for more?

A pufferfish puffed just to fit on the floor,
But then he got stuck, oh the sea's folklore!
With friends all around him, so full of cheer,
They laughed and they rolled without fear.

The narwhals performed a comical song,
While the snappy shrimp joined in, all along.
In this realm where the silly reside,
The creatures find laughter, their joys coincide.

From the tiniest fish to the great whale's calls,
Their joy fills the currents, it dances and sprawls.
Beneath the waves, in this magical space,
Is a funny world, a bubbly embrace!

Echoes from the Ocean Floor

A crab clutched a sandwich, oh what a sight,
He danced with the seaweed, late into night.
"I'm on a diet!" he said with a cheer,
While plump fish around him stuffed chips and beer.

Starfish wore sunglasses, looking so grand,
While turtles played poker with shells in their hands.
The jellyfish twirled in a wobbly ballet,
As clams cheered them on, wrinkled pearls in display.

A dolphin laughed loud, making waves in a groove,
As the sea urchin boogied, trying to move.
The octopus juggled some sea cucumbers,
And everyone joined in, laughing like dancers.

With barnacles quipping, they made quite a show,
Down here in the depths, life's never too slow.
They'll throw you a party, just follow the sound,
Echoes of laughter, oh what fun abound!

Dance of the Celestial Fishes

Fishes in tuxedos, ready to sway,
Their tails all aflutter, in ocean ballet.
A goldfish with bling overflows with delight,
As starfish applaud with their arms waving bright.

The guppies spin fast, like whirlwinds of glee,
While seahorses judge, sipping kelp-infused tea.
A clownfish recites a comedy skit,
The crowd in the coral is loving his wit.

A grouper gets tangled in his own shiny tie,
As a flatfish just blinks, feeling shy oh so shy.
Bubbles rise up like laughter so clear,
In this undersea dance, fun's always near.

When seaweeds are twirling, and the waves start to hum,
You'll find all the critters are having some fun.
A conch plays the trumpet, to wrap up the night,
In the dance of the fishes, all feels just right!

Secrets of the Submerged Realm

An eel in a tux, whispers secrets so sly,
"Why don't fish play piano? Make waves when they try!"
A pufferfish puffed, cracking jokes with a grin,
As turtles debated who might win the spin.

Clams hid their pearls, slinging gossip like darts,
While shrimps plotted mischief, with pranks and playful arts.
The flounder sought wisdom in a gull's old fable,
While sea cucumbers lounged, feeling quite stable.

A mermaid dropped by, with jokes in her net,
"Why don't fish use Facebook? It's hard to upset!"
Giggling, they swayed to the ebb and the flow,
In this sunken realm where the laughter would grow.

With secrets they whisper, and pranks they devise,
Each twist from the current brings smiles to their eyes.
Join in the fun, take a plunge, if you dare,
In this whimsical world, you'll find laughter to share!

Serenity in Saltwater Shadows

In saltwater shadows, the fun never stops,
With jellyfish jiving and sea snails in flops.
A hermit crab scuttles with shoes far too wide,
As fish throw confetti, all laughing with pride.

"What's the best dance?" the anemone asked,
"The shimmy, the splashes, a wiggly task!"
Octopuses winked with eight arms all in play,
Creating a whirlpool that swept all away.

The stingrays wallowed on pillows of sand,
While dolphins made bubbles, a splashy demand.
Surprises abound in this watery realm,
Where smiles float freely, as laughter is helm.

So come join the party, under shadows so bright,
Where every creature swims with pure delight.
In the ebb and the flow, where friends gather near,
The joy of the ocean is what we hold dear!

Beneath the Shimmering Veil

A fish in a tuxedo, looking quite neat,
Swims past a crab with two left feet.
They dance and they twirl, a comical sight,
With bubbles that burst in giggles of light.

A starfish with shades is chilling all day,
While seahorses gossip in a silly way.
Octopus chefs whip up dishes so fine,
But nobody knows what's truly divine!

Clams play the drums on colorful shells,
While jellyfish light up like joyous bells.
A sea cucumber rolls in, causing a scene,
Waving hello, in this underwater dream!

With laughter that ripples in currents so bright,
The ocean's a carnival, pure delight.
Each wave that comes crashing, a tickle or tease,
In this world of wonder, we giggle with ease.

Journeys through Kelp Forests

In forests of kelp where the sea turtles roam,
With mermaids who pick flowers and make them their home.
A dolphin jokes loudly, 'I'm the best swimmer!'
While fish in a bubble laugh, 'You're a beginner!'

A sardine parade, oh such a grand show,
Reef fish in tuxedos put on quite the glow.
They waltz through the waves with a splash and a flip,
It's a swimming gala aboard a sea trip!

Eels in a conga, they wiggle and sway,
While plankton do cartwheels, making a display.
The starry night deep, with bioluminescent,
Turns every sea creature into something pleasant.

As jellyfish dance with their tentacles free,
A coral rock band plays a symphony!
With all of this fun, who could ever feel blue?
In kelp's swaying arms, there's joy for me and you.

When the Sea Sings Softly

When the waves hum a tune, the lobsters prance,
Dancing in circles, they take a big chance.
A pufferfish smiles, puffing out with pride,
To sing along sweetly, joy cannot hide!

With rhythm and bubbles, the urchins will sway,
While squids draw doodles that brighten the bay.
The conch shell's horn gives a raucous call,
Calling for sea creatures, one and all!

Tangled in seaweed, a flounder does charm,
With jokes that he tells, they cause quite the alarm!
A stingray's slow glide brings giggles galore,
As fishes all ponder, 'What's humor for?"

The ocean's a stage, with laughter as sound,
Where every sea creature's quirks do abound.
Together they frolic, in harmony's gleam,
In laughter so soothing, we drift in a dream.

Reflections in the Tidal Pools

In pools of bright water, the crabs hold court,
Sharing their stories, a comical sport.
With one striped like candy, oh what a sight,
His throwback dance moves make everyone bright!

Tiny fish ponder their reflections so neat,
'How do I look?' says one, as he tries to compete.
With a flick of his fin, he attempts to impress,
But slips on a seaweed, oh what a mess!

Anemones giggle as they sway on the sand,
While starfish flip over, a clumsy band.
The tide ebbs and flows, a whimsical game,
As creatures reinvent their reflections, not shame!

So when you stroll past where the pools dance and play,
Join in the laughter, let worries drift away.
For life's but a splash in this watery show,
Where humor is boundless, as the tides ebb and flow.

Dance of the Siren's Song

Bubbles burst with giggling glee,
A fish in a tutu, oh what a sight!
Octopus twirls, just like a bee,
Jellyfish glow in the disco light.

Clams clap their shells, keeping the beat,
A crab does the cha-cha on the sand!
Sea turtles tap with webbed little feet,
As the mollusks form a merry band.

Starfish stomp, a silly parade,
With seaweed wigs, no one looks shy!
A whale in a hat, not quite afraid,
Waves by as he sings a whale's lullaby.

The party goes on 'til the break of dawn,
Fish laugh and dance, what a sight to see!
In the moon's glow, the fun's never gone,
Under the waves, all are wild and free.

Aquatic Reveries

Dolphins play peek-a-boo with shells,
A lobster's jokes cause quite a splash!
Coral reefs ring with silly bells,
As mermaids giggle and make a mad dash.

Small fish race, they're quite the sight,
Flapping their fins like they're in a race!
Crabs crack up at their silly plight,
As sea cucumbers join the chase.

A seahorse spins like a top on a line,
While barnacles boast of their ocean fame!
Clams try to dance but just can't align,
Creating a scene that's hard to tame!

With barnacle bands and bubbles galore,
Every creature joins in on the fun!
Laughter and joy by the ocean's shore,
In this crazy undersea run!

Whispers from the Abyss

An anglerfish winks with a glowy tease,
While shrimps in tuxedos take center stage!
Blowfish puff up with giggles and wheeze,
As eels tell jokes, turning the page.

Cranky crabs fuss over their shells,
Fiddling and faddling, such petulant plight!
Nudibranchs lounge where the water swells,
Living life large, oh what a delight!

Deep-sea divers in flippers so bright,
Clownfish juggle seaweed with flair!
Pufferfish puff as laughter takes flight,
Turning each moment into a fair!

In dark waters where whispers abound,
Tales of giggles and sparkles grow!
For even in depths where mischief is found,
The ocean's humor puts on a show!

Currents of Forgotten Tales

A narwhal brags with a ridiculous grin,
With tales of adventures that stretch for miles.
Seahorses laugh, a colorful spin,
As they tell stories with curious styles.

Old pirates sing of treasure most grand,
While gobies dance at the bottom of lore!
Merfolk on surfboards play in the sand,
Splashing about, who could ask for more?

Whiskered seal pups chase after their tails,
While fish wear glasses, looking quite bright!
Anemones sway and shuffle in gales,
Under the ripples, they party all night!

In the whirlpools of laughter, tales intertwine,
The ocean's charm is a treasure so rare!
Bringing forth memories like sweet, salty wine,
In the depths where the playful spirits dare!

Blue Veils and Fractured Light

In waters where the fish do dance,
A crab once took a bold romance.
He wore a tux, a sight to see,
While trying hard to sip his tea.

The octopus in shades of blue,
Said, "Crustacean, what's wrong with you?"
"You can't wear that with all these waves,
You'll end up in the ocean's graves!"

A shark then swam to steal the show,
With disco moves, he stole the flow.
The seaweed swayed, a vibrant crowd,
Cheering for the sea's dance loud!

And somewhere, bubbles made a scene,
As seahorses twirled, oh so keen.
With laughter echoing, oh so free,
The ocean's party, a sight to see!

A Medley of Shells and Waves

A clam was playing hide-and-seek,
With starfish trying hard to peek.
"Hey, don't you close that shell on me!"
"It's too dark here, I cannot see!"

The waves then splashed with all their might,
While crabs would frolic, full of delight.
Anemones waved with glee and cheer,
As dolphins danced and cracked a beer!

And jellyfish, with graceful glow,
Played tag with seaweed, what a show!
"Catch me if you can," they go,
Floating in currents, ebb and flow.

The seashells laughed, both loud and proud,
As the tide made a raucous sound.
With every wave, a tale to weave,
In ocean's laughter, we believe!

Where the Light Meets the Dark

A nightfish donned a sparkly hat,
And challenged shadows, just like that.
"Come out and play, let's start a ruckus!"
While sea urchins sighed, "Oh, please, muss!"

The murky depths were quite a stage,
With angler fish acting their age.
"Let's have a dance-off!" they all cried,
While sleepy crabs rolled, then pried.

A disco ball of glowing lights,
Drew in the whales for dance delights.
And eels teased with their wiggly ways,
As sharks muttered, "What a funny haze!"

But all it took, a little spark,
To brighten corners, banish dark.
With giggles floating, all around,
The underwater fun was found!

Tides of Memory and Time

Old turtles tell tales of days gone by,
With catchy quotes that make you sigh.
"Back in my day, we swam so fast!"
As fishy friends just laughed and gasped.

A whale with wisdom, deep and wide,
Said, "Life's a wave, just ride, don't hide!"
The clownfish laughed, a vibrant hue,
"That's easy for you, with all that blue!"

A sea cucumber chimed in, quite wise,
"Time flows on, like tides that rise!"
But all the fun, in jest would mix,
As everyone joined in silly tricks.

With memories swirling in ocean's chime,
We danced through water, our laughs in rhyme.
Each tide that came brought tales of cheer,
And in that joy, we held them dear!

The Choreography of Sea Creatures

A crab in a tux, quite the sight,
Dances sideways with all its might.
Fish in top hats swim and twirl,
Underwater, they spin, swirl, and whirl.

Octopuses juggle, what a feat!
With wiggly arms, they can't be beat.
Sea horses prance in a wavy line,
Joining the fun, feeling so fine.

Starfish clapped, what a round of applause!
With five-armed cheers, they caught the cause.
Anemones swayed to the beat of the swell,
In this underwater cabaret, all is well.

Just leap in the waves, don't be shy,
Join the dance, give it a try.
With laughter and bubbles all around,
In the deep blue, joy can be found.

Echoes from Beneath the Surface

A dolphin's burst of giggles is heard,
As waves ride high like playful birds.
Clownfish chuckle with painted grins,
Telling tall tales of their ocean sins.

The octopus whispers jokes so sly,
With a wink from its eye, oh my, oh my!
Shrimps join in, with a bubble or two,
Every giggle a burst of oceanic goo.

Turtles chuckle as they glide slow,
Bored of the currents, they swim to and fro.
"Why did the fish cross the reef?" they tease,
"To find the best seaweed with ease!"

Echoes of laughter bounce all around,
In the layers of blue, joy's abound.
Join the fun, let your giggles free,
For beneath the waves, it's all jollity.

Reflections in a Tide Pool

In a tide pool, salty laughter blooms,
With hermit crabs peeking from shells like rooms.
Barnacles giggle as they hold on tight,
"Life's a splash, so let's take flight!"

Seaweeds dance in the ocean's light,
Tickling the fish, what a funny sight!
Starfish ponder the meaning of a flip,
"Why do we land and what is this trip?"

Snails slide by, in colorful shells,
With whispers of humor from their small wells.
"Race you to the next algae feast!" they say,
Chasing each other in a slippery play.

These tiny wonders, all full of glee,
Prove that laughter's the key to be free.
In every splash, there's fun to explore,
In the tide pool's embrace, forevermore.

The Embrace of Ocean Mist

The surf laughs loudly as it rolls in,
Spraying the fish, inviting a spin.
Cuddled tight in a jellyfish hug,
A sea turtle whirls in a water drug.

Waves tickle crabs on their sandy shore,
"Stop it, you wave!" they scuttle and roar.
The playful sea breeze has come to play,
As sea lions bark, "We've found our way!"

Splashing and giggling, they tumble about,
Caught in the joy, there's never a doubt.
With seagulls swooping in laughter and song,
The ocean's embrace makes us feel strong.

So dive in deep, let your worries wash,
In the embrace where all creatures posh.
With every ripple and wave or mist,
Funny moments are too hard to resist.

Secrets of the Coral Reefs

An octopus juggles shells with glee,
While fish swim round like a bumblebee.
A crab scuttles, wearing a top hat,
Says, 'Silly fish, what's up with that?'

Bright corals giggle in colors grand,
Swaying to music from a clownfish band.
A turtle laughs as he takes a nap,
Dreaming of jelly where weird crabs clap.

Eels play peek-a-boo in their cozy caves,
Bubbles rise high, like frothy waves.
Starfish throw a party on the ocean floor,
While seahorses twirl, always wanting more!

In this underwater world of fun,
Who knew sea life could be such a pun?
So if you dive deep, don't be too shy,
Join in the laughter, let your spirits fly!

A Symphony of Salt and Waves

The seaweed sways like it's got the groove,
As dolphins dance, making their moves.
Clownfish are laughing, wearing big grins,
Singing with bubbles, they're in for wins!

A pufferfish pops to join in the jam,
While a nearby sea turtle snaps a quick slam.
The starfish applaud with bright, shiny arms,
Mimicking musicians, with all their charms.

Squid ink spills like silly confetti,
As the kraken strums on a coral jetty.
Anemones sway, with flow and delight,
While walruses whistle into the night.

A chorus of gulls join the sweet song,
'Round here, we all know we belong!
So grab a fin, or just clap your hands,
This salty symphony, oh how it stands!

Moonlit Reflections on Water

Beneath the moon, the fish all flirt,
With wriggling tails and a little spurt.
A crab in sunglasses throws a cool look,
'Under this moonlight, you could write a book!'

The jellies glow, like lamps in the night,
As shrimps do the cha-cha, what a sight!
A dolphin jumps high, tries to touch the sky,
Flipping and flopping with an earnest sigh.

Starfish twinkle, stacked up like pies,
While seashells gossip in whispers and sighs.
'What's that splash?' the sea cucumbers cry,
'Oh just a new fish, giving it a try!'

Laughter bubbles up, echoing with glee,
As creatures of twilight dance merrily.
So float with the tide, let spontaneity flow,
In this moonlit ballet, let your worries go!

The Stillness of Sunken Time

In a sunken ship, a ghost fish roams,
Looking for treasure and lost, golden homes.
A seahorse takes charge, with a captain's flair,
Directing the search—'Where's the gold, I swear!'

Barnacles gossip, stuck on the wall,
'Did you hear the tale of the last fishball?'
A clam's late-night joke was seriously lame,
Yet everyone laughed—these waters aren't tame!

The octopus spins tales of fish who swam fast,
Claiming they saw things that just couldn't last.
But as bubbles burst, and giggles ensue,
Time stands still in this watery zoo.

Amid the wrecks, there's a party divine,
Where every creature shares laughs over brine.
So if you should venture to depths so sublime,
Join in the fun, for it's just the right time!

Lullaby of the Ocean's Heart

Bubbles dance in a wavy tune,
A fish in a top hat, singing at noon.
Turtles glide by in shoes too tight,
They trip and they tumble, what a silly sight!

Octopus plays the drums with flair,
While clams wear pajamas, sitting in pairs.
A jellyfish waltzes, all floaty and grand,
With seaweed confetti, it's a party unplanned!

Starfish in shades, sunbathing with glee,
A school of bright minnows, doing the bee.
The coral is laughing, it wobbles and sways,
In this wacky world, it's a fishy soiree!

So close your eyes, let the waves sing a tune,
Dream of a dolphin who dances with the moon.
In this aquatic playground, laughter ensues,
Where everyone's silly, and fun's on their cruise!

Coral Dreams and Tide's Caress

In the depths where the colors collide,
A crab in a crown tries to take a ride.
With pajamas of coral, he struts with pride,
The fish all giggle, oh, what a guide!

Seahorses strut in their fanciest bow ties,
While clams in their shells spin tales of surprise.
With bubbles for laughter, the tide rolls along,
In this watery world, everyone's strong!

Jellybeans glow in the soft ocean light,
While squids play tag through the shimmering night.
Anemones cheer as the sea turtles race,
Each splash is a giggle, in this bright space!

Crustaceans breakdance, shells clicking in cheer,
A conch shell DJ spinning tunes we can hear.
Oh, what a party, with friends all around,
In this underwater joy, pure laughter is found!

The Ocean's Secret Garden

In a garden of kelp where the bright colors play,
A lobster in shades hip-hops away.
With flip-flops of foam and a shell on his back,
He groves to the rhythms of an octo with snare.

Clownfish are giggling, a joke they'll unveil,
A sea-urchin chuckles, with spikes that won't fail.
The seaweed's a jester, it tickles the fins,
These playful sea creatures are up for some wins!

Dancing through bubbles, it's a myriad fest,
Where the starfish prance, feeling simply the best.
Anemones wave like they're holding hands tight,
As seahorses stroll in the shimmering light!

With sea songs and laughter, the waves echo by,
The wonders beneath, oh my, how they fly!
In this secret garden where humor runs deep,
Even the mermaids are giggling in sleep!

Beneath the Shimmering Surface

Beneath the surface where the laughter flows,
A fish wears a tie that sparkles and glows.
With bubbles and giggles, a grand parade starts,
As clownfish juggle with watery arts.

A narwhal in glasses is reading a book,
While a lobster in sneakers prepares for a cook.
With salty sea snacks and jokes to be spun,
The ocean's a circus, where laughter runs fun!

Crabs tap dance lightly on soft sandy floors,
And a pufferfish stands by the open sea doors.
He pops when he tickles, he laughs with delight,
Beneath the shimmer, everything feels right!

So if you should wander where the fishes play,
You'll find them all dancing, come join the array.
In this whimsical world, full of comedy bliss,
Let's share in the joy of the ocean's sweet kiss!

www.ingramcontent.com/pod-product-compliance
Lightning Source LLC
Chambersburg PA
CBHW060143230426
43661CB00003B/541